A History of Oldfield Consolidated School 1962-2017

School Section #98
Enfield, Nova Scotia

Including an outline of the story of schooling in Goffs, Oldham, Oakfield, and the 'border district' of Enfield, NS, from 1820 to 2017

John N. Grant

Quarter Castle Publishing
where imagination is magic
Nova Scotia, Canada

Copyright ©John N. Grant 2018

ISBN: 978-1-927625-30-9
Format and design by Diane Tibert

Quarter Castle Press
1787 Highway 2
Milford Station, Nova Scotia, B0N1Y0 Canada

All rights reserved. Unless otherwise indicated, all images are the property of the author. No part of this publication may be reproduced or used in any form or by any means – graphic, electronic or mechanical, including photocopying - or by any information storage or retrieval system without the prior written permission of the publisher. Any requests for photocopying, recording, taping or information storage of any part of this book shall be directed to Quarter Castle Publishing, 1787 Highway 2, Milford, NS, B0N 1Y0. This applies to classroom use as well.

Contents

Acknowledgements/Dedication	iv
The Official Opening	1
Schooling in Oakfield-Grand Lake	4
Schooling in Goffs	6
Schooling in the Enfield Border Section	8
Schooling in Oldham	8
School Consolidation	10
OCS Interior Hallway	12
School Consolidation: Role of the Trustees	12
School Consolidation: Role of the Municipal School Board	14
Consolidation Achieved	16
Oldfield Consolidated School in the 1960s	17
OCS Old Front Door	19
Conversations with Students and Teachers	20
Trustee's Activities	24
The Creation of the School Advisory Council	25
Contributions of School Volunteers	27
School Administration	29
Teachers	31
Students	31
Fire Truck at OCS	33
Conclusion	33
Notes	35
Appendix I	39
Bibliography	40
About the Author	43

Acknowledgements/Dedication

I thank all who assisted me with this project. Many of you are indicated in the notes or elsewhere and to you, and to those not otherwise mentioned, I appreciate your help. Special thanks to the 2016-2017 administration and staff at Oldfield Consolidated School, including Principal Brendon MacGillivray, Vice-Principal Rebecca Campbell, and school secretary, Shelly Crowell, who tolerated my unscheduled visits and kindly provided me with the resources that were available. Thanks also to the *Weekly Press* that accommodated my research as did the Halifax Municipal Archives, the Public Archives of Nova Scotia, the Enfield Heritage Center, and, as always, the Elmsdale Library for unfailing courtesy and support. In addition, I greatly appreciate the contribution of Diane Tibert and Quarter Castle Publishing for bringing the manuscript together and shepherding it into existence.

This work is dedicated to those who have committed themselves to this school and who, as teachers, administrators, and volunteers, have served it well. It is further dedicated to its students and especially to those dearest to me, Julia, Heather, and Andrew Grant.

The Official Opening

On Wednesday evening, 1 May 1963, almost 100 people attended the formal opening of the new Oldfield Consolidated School on Hall's Road, Enfield. The ceremony was chaired by Councillor Mary T. King-Myers, and Lt. Col. Kendrick C. Laurie of nearby Oakfield was the guest speaker. The students of the new six-room school, already in regular use, also participated in the opening by performing "a number of musical selections." The ceremonial presentation of the school's keys saw them passed from the school's builder to the representative of Halifax County and then to the district school board. They were then received by J. Douglas Fleming, the Chair of the local Board of School Trustees, who presented them to the school's first principal, Mrs. Jean McManaman. The school's plaque and a Union Jack were also given to the school during the ceremonies which were opened and closed by the prayers of local clergy.[1]

The organizers of the official opening ceremony of Oldfield Consolidated, and no doubt Principal McManaman was involved, demonstrated a delicate hand. The ratepayers of the Oakfield School Section had been the least convinced of the benefit of consolidation and many were actively disappointed when the new school was not built in Grand Lake. It is very likely, therefore, that the ceremony was designed to promote reconciliation. The new school section was designated as number 98, the same as the former Oakfield Section and the selection of Colonel Laurie as the guest speaker was prudent. Laurie, who was a member and former chair of the board of governors of Dalhousie University and a distinguished citizen, was an excellent choice under any circumstances. His intimate identification with Oakfield-Grand Lake made his selection inspired. Laurie's agreement to appear suggested he supported the committee's intent. The chair of the meeting, Counsellor Mary Teresa King-Myers was from the Wellington area. She was elected to Halifax County Council in 1937 and was the first female counsellor in Canada. She held the position until 1949, when she resigned because she moved out of the district. She was especially interested in health and education and when she returned home, she was re-elected to Council and served from 1957 to 1967.[2]

Oldfield Consolidated School was built to replace the schoolhouses in the school sections of Oldham, Goffs, and Oakfield and provide for the Border Section of Enfield in Halifax County. The four school sections that came together in 1961-62 had very different histories. Oakfield began as a great estate in the tradition of the English landed gentry, while Oldham was a result of the discovery of gold. Goffs (Old Guysborough Road), on the other hand, was a typical Nova Scotian rural community economically based in farming and forestry and more similar to the Enfield Border Section than it was to either of the other two.

OCS Plaque

The plaque, unveiled at the official opening, was moved during renovations, but is again affixed to the wall of Oldfield Consolidated School.

Schooling in Oakfield-Grand Lake

The Oakfield School District was named in honour of the estate and community established by Major (later Lieutenant-General) John Wimburn Laurie (1835-1912). Laurie arrived in Nova Scotia in 1861, and he married Francis Robie Collins at St. Paul's Church in Halifax in 1863. Her father, Enos Collins (1774-1871), was an entrepreneurial businessman who accumulated one of the greatest fortunes in British North America, and her mother, Margaret Haliburton Collins, was a member of the provincial gentry, a descendent of both Sir Breton Haliburton, Chief Justice of Nova Scotia, and Charles Inglis, the first Lord Bishop of the province.[3] Collins apparently hoped the young couple would settle near Windsor where he owned land, but they set their hearts on Grand Lake. In 1865, Laurie purchased 500 acres of land there and called the estate 'Oakfield'. One of his descendants later recorded that it "was a shock to their many friends in society when Col. and Mrs. Laurie closed their house on Morris Street [Halifax] and moved 25 miles away to the house they were building in the woods on the shores of Grand Lake."[4] The closest settlement was Fletcher's Bridge, which Laurie eventually renamed Wellington in honour of the great British war hero and political leader, Arthur Wellesley, (1769-1852), the Duke of Wellington.

Oakfield grew to become more than the name of the house and grounds. Laurie hired labourers and the land was cleared. As Clara Dennis reported in 1937, "Field after field of twenty-five acres each was laid out by the Major. ... They open one into another and are surrounded by stone walls sheltered by rows of trees. And such stone walls! Over four feet high and six feet thick they are, all built of stone taken from the Major's land."[5] Despite Laurie's military and other duties elsewhere, he did not lose interest in his Oakfield estate.

As years went on, Oakfield developed. Land was added on both sides of the lake, cottages were built, each having field, barn, and woodlot, and in 1873, Col. Laurie came back from a visit to England with a number of Devonshire men. Their families were settled into the cottages, a school was built, the church had been constructed in 1866, and for years Oakfield was an English settlement in the backwoods.[6]

Oakfield's first schoolhouse was constructed in 1874-75, one of the seven new schools built that year in Halifax County. They were described by Hinkle Condon, the county's inspector of schools, as being "large, convenient and well furnished, and a credit to their respective sections."[7] That schoolhouse apparently served the community until the mid-1940s when a new "modern two-room wooden building" replaced the old schoolhouse.[8] In 1959-60, the school continued to serve its community with two teachers and sixty-five students in grades primary to eight.[9] The Oakfield School Section #98 may have been among the leaders in the involvement of women in school government. While female teachers had been in the majority since the later 1800s, that was not the case at the management level. However, in his 1924-25 report to the provincial authorities, Inspector Graham Creighton noted that "beginning has been made in the appointment of women to the rural boards. Miss Margaret Laurie has been on the trustees board of the Oakfield section for a number of years and has been instrumental in effecting a very great improvement in the condition and character of the school."[10] But, whatever the 'condition and character' of the school in Oakfield, it was swept up in the school consolidation movement, enabled by better roads, school buses, and the enormous expectations of the 1960s of public schooling into the new Oldfield Consolidated School.

Schooling in Goffs

A new school in the Goffs School Section #44 was opened in 1891. That year, Inspector Condon reported that "Goffs, a poor and scattered section with only 20 children from 5 to 15 years of age, has now a suitable house belonging to the section," a building which might have replaced a school built between 1872 and 1879. The land grants in the "Guysborough Road (Goffs) area began in 1784," but it is less clear when actual settlement began. However, "in 1812 three young brothers by the name of Goff left Ireland for Nova Scotia" and one of them, Thomas, was granted 100 acres of land on the Guysborough Road. By the early 1840s, Thomas and his wife, Eleanor Holland Goff, had settled on their grant accompanied by many of their children. The family also ran an "Inn familiarly known as Goffs, a name which became adopted for the local village." The Goffs Inn, located directly across from the school, was a stage stop and in 1879 "also became the area's post office which carried on at the same house until 1969." The Goff family was not the first to settle in the region, and the small community, like most in rural Nova Scotia grew or diminished in response to local conditions and external pressures.[11]

There were several schools spaced along the Old Guysborough Road and the Goffs "Academy', as it was apparently referred to locally, was one of them. Old Guysborough Road historians Noreen Gray and Annie Smith suggested that the first school in Goffs was opened as early as the 1830s. However, in the school year 1959-1960, the one-room school at Goffs served only grades primary to three with a total enrolment of 26 students. By1961, the number of students at Goffs had increased to 28 in a building designed for 24. In response to the over-crowding, the Municipal School Board moved the Grade 3 class to the Oldham School and added a second teacher at Oldham in a split-shift. The Goffs and Oldham students in grades 5 to 8 were moved to the Oakfield (Grand

Lake) School, which was also over-crowded. The post-war baby-boom had swollen the school population and forced school authorities to make decisions that were not always popular.[12]

The memories of the 'good-old-days' in the one-room school have prevailed, and Gray and Smith tell the story of one of the most remembered features of the site of the 1891 school building at Goffs. They wrote:

> A story that always seems to surface when we talk to the former pupils and teachers of Goff school concerns a very large silver poplar which appears in many of the old school pictures. The tree, planted on Arbour Day, 1907 by the teacher and pupils of Goffs School, lived rather precariously for its first few years. It seems the boys, probably to tease the girls, would pull it up. The girls would then replant it. Though this was supposed to have happened many times, the tree did not receive any permanent damage and survived, towering over the small one-room school for some seventy years. Swings were tied to its lower branches and generations of Goffs children have many fond memories of this tree which remained keeping vigil beside the old school.

After the school was closed, the building served as a community hall and then became part of the first fire department building, when the old tree had to be removed.[13]

Progress caught up with Goffs when the decision was made to replace the old Halifax City airport and by "1960 much of the original village was buried under slabs of concrete that made the Halifax International Airport".[14] With a total population of 137 in 1956 and with the incursion of the airport, as well as parental concern about schooling, the replacement of the Goffs School by the new Oldfield Consolidated was likely seen, at least by some, as a step forward.

Schooling in the Enfield Border Section

A 'Border Section' school district was one that straddled a county line and had students of both counties attending a school in one of them. The families who lived in the Enfield Border Section sent their children to school in nearby Enfield, Hants County which, after 1943, was the E. H. Horne School built by Edmund and Anna Horne to benefit his home community. In 1957-58, the E. H. Horne School had six teachers and 175 students, including those from Halifax County. The Halifax School Board paid tuition to the host Board for their attendance. The creation of Oldfield Consolidated meant the pupils attended school in Halifax County instead and thus eliminated some of the bureaucracy of cross-county schooling.

Schooling in Oldham

The history of Oldham as a community dates from 1861 with the discovery of gold. The lure of wealth attracted investment and employment, and mining began in 1862 with eight crushers in operation by 1863. Within the community there was, apparently, "considerable friction with respect to the name the district should bear." The dispute was settled by Premier Joseph Howe whose visit:

> was made the occasion of a general jollification. Mounting an improvised platform, which had been erected in the vicinity of the first store in the mines, Mr. Howe delivered one of his characteristic addresses, in which he dwelt upon the mineral possibilities of the country, and concluding he counselled a more fraternal feeling among the miners and then announced that he would name the district, Oldham, in honour of the birthplace in England of his ancestors. The unstinted flow of liquid hospitality which was such a feature of mining life at that time, was quite sufficient to render all his

auditors quite willing to accept the name he had chosen for them.[15]

Thereafter, the prosperity of Oldham and the number of people who lived in the mining/school district depended on the output of the mines. In 1908, Oldham had two churches, a general store, a hotel, and a quartz mill for cleansing gold.[16]

The first schoolhouse in Oldham School Section #99 was built in 1866 and replaced by a new building in 1886. That year, Inspector Hinkle Condon reported that it was "well furnished with patent desks as well as first class black boards and new maps." In an era when schools were opened for both winter and summer terms, the new building meant that "the Summer term will be entered upon exceedingly favourable conditions." Inspector Condon was enthusiastic about the new desks, which local school trustees had provided in only twenty-seven of the county's 129 school sections, noting they were a "great improvement on the clumsy, old fashioned ones."[17] Those were obviously good years in Oldham, and the school trustees were financially secure enough to be educationally progressive. Generations of boys and girls sat in those desks until the students, in their turn, either went to work in the mines, the woods, or joined the migration to employment. Some of them, especially the young women, became teachers themselves while others joined the exodus to the 'Boston states' and elsewhere.

The glory days of gold mining at Oldham had passed by the middle of the twentieth-century. In 1956 the population was 155, and the sites of the mines, crushers, stores, hotels, and many of the homes were marked by foundation stones and lonely lilac bushes. With the reduction of the tax base and the increased expectation of schools, Oldham, like the other school sections involved, accepted that a new consolidated school might better serve the needs of their children.

School Consolidation

However, new schools, especially new consolidated schools are generally not easily created. The arguments of those who did not want change, who feared an increase in taxation, or who prophesied the closure of the local school would mean the death of the community, had to be faced. As compelling as these arguments were, the consolidators could also present a strong case.

Their first argument was that what was happening in the local area was a reflection of what was occurring across the country. In the 1950s "... post-war circumstances created a new interest and unprecedented demands for education among Canadians who more and more saw schooling as the major means of improved opportunity for their children."[18] In Nova Scotia, increased demand for schooling in the years between 1956 and 1963 saw school enrolment increase "from 156,847 to 192,649 and the number of classrooms from 5,208 to 6,943. The number of rural, district, and regional high schools increased by five times; and the replacement of old buildings by consolidated schools reduced the number of one-room schools in operation from 1,100 to less [sic] than 400." In addition, between 1953 and 1963, "the Grade 12 enrolment increased by 136% and the Grade 11 enrolment doubled."[19] These numbers were reflected in Halifax County where "the Board realized that many of the smaller rural schools were in poor condition and rather than spend considerable money on renovations or additions to these old buildings, the Board commenced a program of consolidation in 1956 that continued to 1981 ... under the Halifax County School Board."[20]

In addition, while the social changes that infused the 1960s came later to some communities than others, the world news also affected attitudes about schooling. In 1957 the USSR launched the first satellite (Sputnik I) into space and within months, Sputnik II carried a dog into orbit. The United States responded with the 1958 launch of Vanguard I and the space race was on. In 1961, Yuri Gagarin became the first man in space, to be 'one-upped' by American Neil Armstrong who walked on the moon in 1969. The contest between communist and democratic systems and east and west was such that it "became popular to aver that the safety of the state and the survival of the free world depended upon the schools – particularly upon science and mathematics teachers who were often referred to as 'front-line troops' in the struggle against the Red Menace. For a period of time, opposition to school budgets was unpatriotic."[21] If schooling could save the free world, its influence could be pervasive and by the 1960s, the:

> Popular faith in education … reached religious proportions … . In the minds of some, education became confused with evolution. The schools were expected to provide liberty, equality, and fraternity, to end crime, abolish welfare, guarantee good jobs, cultivate the mind, liberate the spirit, underwrite democracy, elevate moral standards, cure (or prevent) mental illness, guarantee happiness, stimulate inquiry, manufacture wise men, combat alcoholism, protect the public health, ensure a healthy sex life, and end premarital sex and pregnancy. Education, someone discovered, was not an expense at all, but an investment.[22]

With expectations like these, and with the full support of the provincial school authorities, it is little wonder our local single section one- and two-room schools were closed and replaced by the Oldfield Consolidated School.

OCS Interior Hallway

The end of another busy day at Oldfield Consolidated School, but tomorrow the familiar halls will be teeming with students again.

School Consolidation: Role of the Trustees

With the provincial Department of Education and the Municipal School Board clearly in favour of school consolidation, public school inspectors regularly advocated the plan to local Trustees. The role of School Trustees was to run the local school. Elected by the ratepayers (taxpayers) of the school section, Trustees were originally responsible for ensuring a school building was constructed and maintained, hiring the teacher(s), collecting the school tax to pay the teacher's salary and other school expenses, encouraging attendance, and supporting discipline. Gradually, however, authority over schooling was centralized into the hands of the municipal bureaucracy. For example, in 1955, the provincial government increased the authority of the Municipal School Boards by transferring the power to appoint teachers to the Board. However, the Trustees still had to be convinced to close local schools before consolidation could take place.

In 1959, Margaret Garrison, who had served as Secretary to the Goffs School Board of Trustees, was a 'permissive' teacher in the Goffs School between January and June. Because she was an untrained beginner, the local supervisor of schools, E. T. Marriott, helped her prepare lessons for her students. Apparently, they also discussed "the unsatisfactory situation at Goffs School and also the Enfield Border Section since our tax dollars were going to pay tuition for those pupils to Hants County." In Mrs. Garrison's memory, the local schools continued to deteriorate "until Jan. 1961 when the situation became impossible", a problem that was evident throughout Nova Scotia, especially in the rural schools. In response, a meeting of the Trustees was held in the Goffs School in January 1961, and the Trustees from Oldham as well as representatives from Enfield (Halifax County) were invited to attend. Also in attendance was E. T. Marriott, representing the municipal school board. After some discussion, on Marriott's suggestion, it was agreed they would attend

> ... a second meeting when all interested ratepayers should be present. This meeting was held in Oldham school, it being the largest building available. The date was Jan. 30, 1961. At this time Mr. Marriott felt that Grand Lake should be asked if they were willing to consolidate with the other sections as it would be more satisfactory educationally and financially. A third meeting was called for Feb. 17, 1961 at which both Mr. Marriott and Mr. Perry [Keith Perry, Inspector of Schools for Halifax County] were present as well as the trustees and ratepayers from Grand Lake. After some heated discussion Grand Lake agreed to consolidate.[23]

School Consolidation: Role of the Municipal School Board

Inspector Keith Perry informed the Municipal School Board of these meetings on 1 March 1961. On hearing that Oldham, Goffs, and the Border Section wanted the new school built "in the immediate vicinity of the Enfield-Border Section" and "roughly located about a quarter of a mile off the main highway towards Goffs on what is known as the Post Road," and that Grand Lake wanted it build in Grand Lake, the Board decided that "we should let this situation lie for a while and discuss it at a future meeting." The issue reappeared on the agenda of the 28 March 1961 meeting, and again the Board decided that it "could take no action at this time" and recommended that Mr. Marriott and Mr. Perry meet with the various Trustees and report to the Board.[24]

The April meeting of the Board was informed that the parties had become entrenched in their positions and the Oldham, Goffs, and the Enfield representatives suggested they consolidate and Oakfield could remain apart. This, however, was not acceptable to the Board, and it requested a meeting with the Oakfield Trustees that occurred in early May. The Oakfield Trustees ably argued their case for a Grand Lake site with the added incentive of "property offered by Colonel Laurie to erect this school in Oakfield." In June, the Board received a letter from the Acting Secretary of the combined School Sections of Goffs, Oldham, and the Border Section requesting information about the likelihood of their consolidated school being built and they, in turn, were invited to meet with the Board. In their meeting, the Trustees were "very firm in their stand that a school be built in the immediate vicinity of the Enfield Border Section" and decried what they interpreted as favouritism being shown to Grand Lake. They were assured the Boards only interest was "the best terms of education for all concerned and that a hasty decision cannot be made." Perhaps mollified, if not satisfied, the delegation agreed that students in grades 7 to 9 might be bussed to a proposed junior high school but insisted that "their children from Primary to Grade VI remain in their own area."[25]

In July, a special meeting of the Municipal School Board was held to discuss "the proposed Capital Building Program for September of 1962." Among the decisions made at the meeting was that "a six room [sic] school with capacity to add four rooms be built at Enfield (Halifax County) to serve the School Sections of Oldham, Goff's [sic], Enfield (Halifax County) and Grand Lake."[26] The compromise between the Post Road and Grand Lake sites did not satisfy the Grand Lake ratepayers. In October 1961, the Municipal School Board received a letter reiterating all their arguments and a petition from Grand Lake again requesting the school be built in that community. In balance, the Board also received a letter from Enfield expressing concern "over the letter in the press regarding the steps that have been taken" to have the school built in Grand Lake. The Board, however, had made its decision and directed its secretary to respond to both parties informing them "that the school will be built around the Enfield border area" and that the decision could not be revoked "as the plans are now underway to have the Capital Building Committee to go into the area and look for a possible school site." In a diplomatic response to all parties, the Board thanked everyone for the "extreme interest they have shown concerning the building of this consolidated school, and that they should be commended for their effort."

Between 1956 and 1981, there were twenty-eight school consolidations in Halifax County with 110 school buildings declared surplus, including #44 Goffs, #98 Oakfield, and #99 Oldham on 13 November 1962.[27] As Secretary to the Municipal School Board Clary Briggs explained:

> The consolidations were certainly not easy. The Board held meetings with the ratepayers in each community …

to explain the process of consolidation and to get the consensus of opinion and the vote. Needless to say, many of these meetings were very long, vocal and heated. These difficulties were understood and appreciated by the Board and staff, as they recognized that the people did not want to give in easily because they were losing a very important part of their community.[28]

The agreement of the trustees and ratepayers to consolidate school sections and the Board's decision about the location they considered most central and convenient for students were necessary steps in the process. However, before a new school could be built, a precise location had to be determined and a variety of lots were suggested and investigated before the Hall's Road site was approved. The land purchased for the school was part of the Todd farm which fronted on Highway #2 where the farmhouse (#6615) is still standing. In Mrs. Garrison's words "a great many hours and a lot of mid-night oil was used to finally get things under way." The community meetings, committee meetings, and community attendance at Council meetings, as well as Mrs. Ledwidge's "visit to Warden George Burris at his home in Upper Musquodoboit who was also chairman of the Municipal School Board" all contributed to moving the project forward. The local organizing committee and the early trustees, included Douglas Flemming, Laurie Ledwidge, Dorothy Campbell, Velma Ledwidge, Murray Garrison, and trustees secretary Margaret Garrison, carried much of the responsibility of the community "to provide a good school for their children." The individual who had the longest connection with the school was Velma Ledwidge who served either as an elected trustee or as secretary to the trustees from 1962 to 1996.[29]

Consolidation Achieved

While the official date of the consolidation of the Oldfield School Section #98 was 1 August 1962, the first annual meeting of the ratepayers was held on 8 February 1962. It decided, among other questions, on the name of the new school. A number of names were brought forward and two, Long Lake School suggested by Oscar Conrad and Oldfield by Phyllis Thompson, were put to a vote. The name Oldfield, Phyllis Thompson explained, was derived by extracting 'old' from Oldham and Old Guysborough Road (Goffs) and 'field' from Enfield and Oakfield. A standing vote determined that the new institution would be called Oldfield Consolidated School. The meeting also voted to accept the advice of Inspector Keith Perry and decided its Board of Trustees would consist of five persons, with one representing each of the old school sections (Enfield, Goffs, Oakfield, and Oldham), and one 'floater' or member-at-large, a distribution that remained in place until the trustees were disbanded in 1996.[30]

The Oldfield Consolidated School was designed by architect Lester J. Page and was one of a number of schools in Halifax County built to the same specifications. It was constructed by Merlin Kerr Woodworkers Limited and at the 3 July 1962 meeting of the Municipal School Board, it was "reported that the school would be ready by September of 1962" and apparently it was occupied that month.[31]

Oldfield Consolidated School in the 1960s

The first principal of Oldfield Consolidated School was Jean McManaman. The building consisted of six classrooms which were fully occupied, as was the "crush" area, by students in grades Primary to Eight. The over-crowding was such that in its first year of operation (1962-1963), the Municipal School Board agreed to add two more classrooms. However, in December 1962, the Oldfield Trustees informed the Board that the number of students enrolled demanded that the classes from Primary to Six each needed its own classroom but that grades Seven and Eight "can be combined for this one term." In addition, there were 17 students for "remedial' who also required classroom space. Consequently, the Trustees argued, a minimum of nine classrooms would be required in 1963-1964. Based on these figures, the Oldfield Trustees recommended four classrooms rather than two be approved for September of 1963. The Board agreed and in its annual report to the Halifax County Municipal Council, it noted that: "In November 1962, the Municipal School Board requested an addition of two rooms to the Oldfield Consolidated School. More recent information leads us to believe that this addition would satisfy the needs for only one year and since it appears more economical to build four rooms at one time rather than two additional at close intervals, we are recommending the addition of four rooms rather than two rooms to this school."[32]

Construction proceeded apace, and on 5 June 1963 it was reported that the four-room addition "will be completed by August 15" in time for the 1963-1964 school-year. Although I have not been able to locate the architects plans of the addition, most witnesses agreed it was built on the Hall's Road end of the building. While memory can be capricious, the roof line and other physical evidence support that claim. Consequently, the end door on Hall's Road effectively became the main entrance to the school.

In 1965-1966, Oldfield Consolidated was still a P - 8 school with eight teachers and a total of 229 students. Two hundred and two of them were in the elementary classes with 27 in the junior high (grades 7 and 8). Grade 9 students were bussed to Sidney Stephen High School (est. 1960) in Bedford. By 1967-1968, Oldfield became a P - 6 school as it has been ever since. In that year, however, there was also an Auxiliary Class of 15 students and a total of 220 pupils and a compliment of eight teachers. Graduating students attended L. C. Skerry Junior High School (est. 1963) in Waverley before going on to Sidney Stephen, which had reverted to grades 10 – 12. After 1968, Oldfield students, on the completion of grade 6, entered

George P. Vanier Junior High School (est. 1968) and then progressed to Sidney Stephen High School in Bedford. Later, grades 10, 11, and 12 attended Sackville High School (est. 1972) in Lower Sackville, then Charles P. Allan High School (est. 1979) in Bedford, and still later Lockview High School (est. 2000) in Fall River.[33]

OCS Old Front Door

The 'front door' of the school. Painted red for many years, today Oldfield Consolidated School is blue.

Conversations with Students and Teachers

The five children of the MacDonald family were among the first students to attend Oldfield Consolidated School. The MacDonald farm stretched along the east side of Hall's Road and extended across the land now occupied by the four-lane 102 Highway. Their farmhouse was in the vicinity of Irving 'Big Stop'. Like many rural Enfield (Halifax County) residents, the MacDonald's supplemented their farm income by working in the woods in the winter and commercially fishing the river during the season. When David MacDonald (b. March 1959) was ready to attend school, the family was living on Hall's Road, just across from Oldfield Consolidated. David remembers his school days, his classmates, and his former teachers, including those most likely to give one a rap across the knuckles with a ruler if your attention wandered. He recalls the Christmas concerts, student hi-jinks, and, because he lived so close, going home for dinner rather than eating with his classmates.

For David and his contemporaries, Oldfield Consolidated was brand new and the "big school". While the school population was largely White, there was some racial diversity. The MacDonald's are Mi'kmaw and David recalls the African-Nova Scotian students, primarily from the Guysborough Road, who also attended Oldfield Consolidated. David's educational journey took him to George P. Vanier Junior High School and then to Sackville High. After grade 10, he joined the military for a number of years. David was athletic and played defence for local hockey teams, then the East Hants All Stars, and graduated to the Kitchener (Ontario) Rangers with the rising élite of hockey, including a young Mark Messier. Today, he lives in the family home on Hall's Road and is actively involved in the salt water fishery in south-west Nova Scotia. He also maintains a three-generation tradition of the fishery on the Shubenacadie River that he now pursues with a fourth generation of his family. His first school is always in his sight and he remembers it as a "good school".[34]

Jean McManaman, whose husband Morley was the Station Master in Elmsdale, served as principal until 1970 and is remembered by a fellow teacher as "a lovely person to work with; good to her teachers"; and as being "on their side" in any dispute with the Trustees or parents. Her school had a "good atmosphere" and was a happy place to work.

Lois Mackeil taught at Oldfield Consolidated School for twelve years between 1965 and 1977 and remembers it as some of the best years of her teaching life. Mrs. Mackeil had started teaching when she was seventeen, armed with two months training at the Teachers College and a Temporary Licence. Mrs. Mackeil taught for several years until she and her family moved to Elmsdale where her husband was employed. After being out of the classroom for some time, she was recommended for a position at Oldfield Consolidated as the grade five teacher. During her years there, she taught grades five, three, and two and attended summer school to raise her teaching qualifications. It was an all-female staff during many of those years and they all got along well. The students were "a nice bunch of kids", "good students", and pleasant to work with. Because it was a bus school at a time when not everyone owned a car, after-school and evening activities for students were limited. Lunch time and recess, whenever possible, meant outdoor play for the students and supervision duty for the teachers. In the fall of 1977, Mrs. Mackeil moved to another school but, when she looks back at her life in teaching, it is the years at Oldfield that stand out. In response to why, she simply stated: "I loved it there."[35]

Oldfield Journal

One of various iterations of an Oldfield Consolidated School student newspaper, this one dates from April 1983 with grade 6 student Robin Forrester as editor. It contains reports about school dances, the grade 5 charity group called Teen Angels, sports, musical instruments, Pioneer Day and other special events, as well as a variety of stories written by students of all grades.

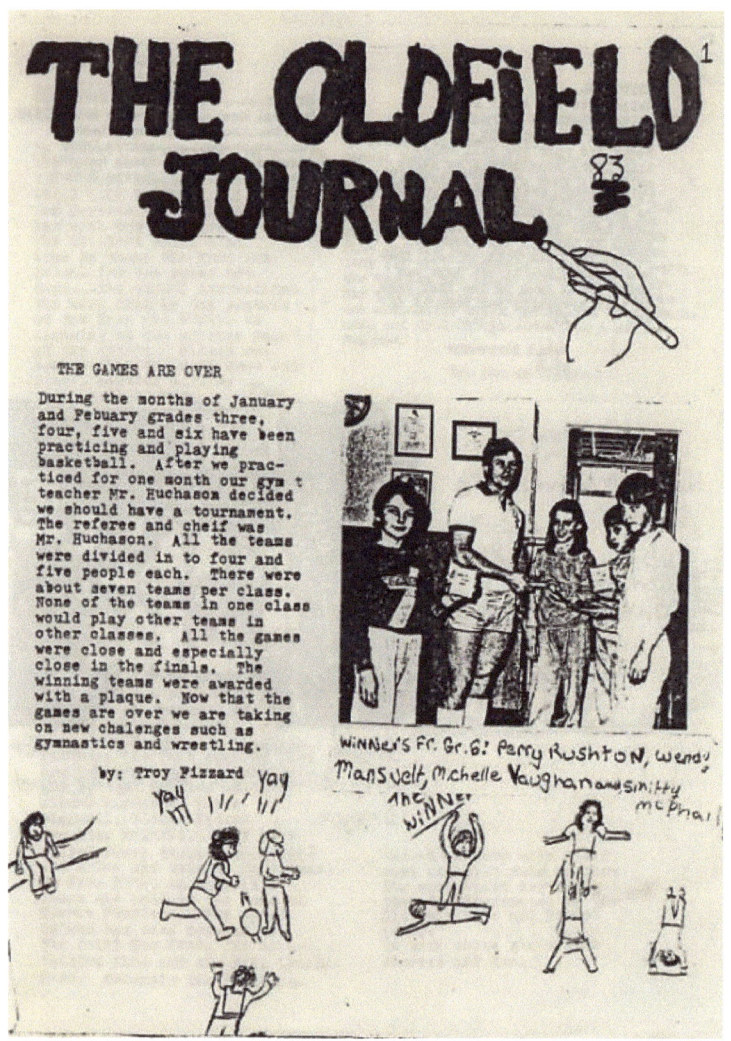

Martha Mills taught at Oldfield Consolidated School for twenty-one years. After graduating from the Nova Scotia Teachers College in 1973 and nine years of teaching experience, she came to Oldfield in 1983 and remained until she retired in 2005. During these years, the school was an important part of her life and she was an important part of the life of the school. Living in the community, she became acquainted with generations of students and parents both inside and outside the classroom. Her teaching life spanned the tenures of six different principals, many teachers, and hundreds of students. Her memories of her years at Oldfield are positive. She reflects that there was a "good mixture of students from different economic and social classes but at school they were nicely integrated."

Mrs. Mills wrote plays for her students that featured the educational theme of the year and integrated a variety of subject matter. Because she lived close to the school, Martha Mills was often there on Saturday with students painting backdrops and otherwise preparing for production. She remembers the staff wrote skits and performed them for the amusement of the students; one presentation devolved into a memorable water fight, much to the chagrin of the caretaker. In later years, in Mrs. Mills' judgment, there was not as much time for socialization because teachers were caught in a web of curriculum overload, program plans, meetings, and paper work. But, she concludes, if she had the opportunity to reorganize her life, there is not much she would change and certainly not her years at Oldfield Consolidated School. Her involvement with the school and teaching did not end with her retirement. Mrs. Mills still occasionally tutors students who need additional instructional time and she served on the School Advisory Council.[36]

Trustee's Activities

The business and the busyness of the school day can disguise the ongoing efforts of school administration to support the schooling of students. School principals, the Board of School Trustees, the School Advisory Council, and other volunteer groups, have all contributed to Oldfield Consolidated School. Sometimes what seem to be minor accomplishments might take years to bring about. For example, the desirability of a school-yard light was recommended by the Trustees in 1982. This agenda item was regularly reintroduced to the Trustees and always supported. However, despite the petitions of the Trustees and the support of school administration, the light was not installed until 1989. The 1982 primary class was in junior high school by the time the issue left the Trustees agenda. The Trustees were regularly involved with the ongoing maintenance of the building. They did 'walk-throughs' and made suggestions about painting, cleaning, and yard litter. They also instigated the "additional parking by the theatre fence" in 1980, and recommended safety rules for the playground. For several years, they advocated for boot and coat racks for the students but when they were built, they "voiced disapproval of the newly installed coat and boot racks which are too short, too high and the lumber is neither sanded nor painted" and at their insistence the alterations were made. In the 1990s, the Trustees argued for the replacement of the roof of the school and for the up-grading of the wiring to meet the needs of the growing use of technology.

The Trustees received regular reports from the principal and responded to complaints from parents about school affairs. They made reluctant decisions about the suspension or expulsion of students and handled complaints about teachers. They were concerned about student success and in the early 1970s, the Trustees discussed how to provide the special services needed by some pupils.[37] Some events activated the school community. In March 1988, "a building permit was issued to the Irving Oil Company to build a truck stop" at the intersection of Highway #2 and Hall's Road. Many of the residents, but not all, were opposed to the "permit because of the proximity to Oldfield Elementary School" and feared for the safety of their children. There was a sometimes rancorous meeting at the school about the issue which was eventually put to rest when Irving Oil located its now well-established business on the other side of the Trans-Canada Highway, well away from Oldfield School.[38]

The Creation of the School Advisory Council

Over the years, the administration of public schools in Nova Scotia became increasingly centralized. Local school boards became larger administrative units and in 1991, the Boards were fully elected. In 1995 the Minister of Education announced plans to restructure public education in Nova Scotia by the creation of six amalgamated school boards and one provincial board (the Conseil Scolaire Acadien Provincial). He also declared the intention to establish school advisory councils to replace the boards of school trustees.

On 15 September 1995, Principal Tom Robson noted in his report to the Oldfield Consolidated School Annual Ratepayers Meeting that the "Department of Education and the School Board is moving towards the establishment of School Advisory Councils for all schools during this school year. ... At the request of the Parent Support Group, and, I hope, the understanding of the Board of Trustees, I am investigating how such a council can be established and the exact terms of reference for its input into the school."[39] The last meeting of the Board of Trustees was held on 1 May 1996. After dealing with the usual business on their agenda, Secretary Velma Ledwidge noted that "No future meetings are planned due to the uncertainty of any future role of the Trustees."[40]

While Principal Robson may have intended to act quickly to establish the School Advisory Council, it was negated when he was transferred from Oldfield Consolidated. He was replaced by Principal Ronald Muir in 1997 and on 11 February 1998, Muir placed a "Public Notice" in the *Weekly Press* advertising the establishment of a School Advisory Council for "Oldfield Elementary School". It advised *Weekly Press* readers that "There will be a meeting of parents and community members at the school on February 26 at 7 P. M. 72 Hall's Road, Enfield" to discuss the formation of the SAC.[41] The records of the early years of the Council are apparently not available, but it is likely safe to assume the Oldfield School Advisory Council was organized as a result of that meeting. The Council is a legally recognized body. It includes the school principal as well as representatives of parents, teachers, support staff, community members and, under some circumstances, students. Its role is to work together to better the quality of education provided by the local school. It is as active as the membership wishes it to be and its attention changes with the concerns of the school and the community. The Oldfield School Advisory Council continues its mission to serve as one of the links between the school and the community. Since 1996, the power over many of the former responsibilities of the Board of School Trustees resides in the hands of school authorities. The important role of the volunteer School Advisory Council is to promote the interest of the school in the community and represent the interest of the community in the school. At Oldfield, it has been actively involved in protecting the school from the establishment of what many deemed unsuitable business neighbours on the lands that border the building and worked to ensure the school itself was not swept away in another round of consolidation.

OCS Ball Field
The ball field at Oldfield Consolidated School

Contributions of School Volunteers

Other volunteer groups, including the Parent Teacher Association and the Home and School Association, have also been active in support of Oldfield Consolidated School. The first computer, a Commodore C-64, was donated to the school by the Home and School in 1985, just a year after the first electric typewriter made its appearance at Oldfield and just before the first 'Xerox' machine. Eventually, the school "converted a former gym supply room to a resource lab and is steadily adding to their computer lab resources." The volunteer parent association raised funds to purchase new equipment and upgrade software, and Oldfield also received two computers from a donation to Halifax Regional Municipality from the Sable Offshore Energy Company.[42] The Parent Support Group was instrumental in the creation of the ball field in the 1980s and 1990s. Individual parents volunteered their time, equipment, and expertise to fill and grade that part of the school grounds. The chain link fence, installed in 1992, was financed by the Municipal School Board as was the final seeding. The Parent Support Group also contributed playground equipment, a service that was more lately duplicated by the Parent Teacher Organization and private donors. Parent volunteers also supported the school library and a great many other school events, including school trips, dental hygiene, and field days. The now nascent Block Parent Program was another volunteer service to the school and over the years, a number of individuals have made contributions including, in the mid-1980s, a gift of a new flag pole for the school and from another, the planters that contributed to a school beautification project supported by the Parent Action Group.

OCS Playground
Part of the playground equipment at Oldfield Consolidated School

School Administration

There were two principals in the first 22 years of the life of Oldfield Consolidated School. In the following 33 years, there have been ten. Each of them brought their professional and personal interest and their willingness to further the education of the students in their care. While individual teachers usually have the longest tenure in a school, the importance of administration cannot be over emphasized as principals tend to set the tone of the school. The early administrators were teaching-principals who had to work their administrative duties around their teaching responsibilities. It was not until 1977 that the Trustees reported that Principal Don Leslie was granted one morning a week for administrative duties. That same year, the new agreement between the Nova Scotia Teachers Union and the Department of Education freed teachers from supervisory duties other than twenty minutes before classes and twenty minutes after class in the afternoon. Because teachers were no longer required to supervise at noontime, the School Board permitted that a 'non-professional' noontime supervisor could be employed at the rate of $3.50 per day. The move to a shorter lunch break and an earlier end to the school day were also, at least in part, prompted by the change in teacher's prescribed duties.

As the responsibilities of the Board of Trustees were reduced, those of the school administration were increased. More and more the management of the whole 'plant', academic, professional, and building maintenance came under the purview of the principal and later of the principal and vice-principal. Support for the administration came in March 1985, when the Trustees were informed that beginning the following year, a school secretary would be employed for three one-half day periods a week. School secretaries, who interact with everyone in any way connected with the operation, generally have their finger on the pulse of the school and contribute greatly to its professional management. This was a big step from the days when an early principal requested a second telephone so he would not have to sprint from his classroom to his office every time a call was received.

One of the regular administrative concerns was school enrollment. While Jean McManaman had to deal with over-crowding, later principals have watched the numbers fall. In September 1978, Principal Leslie reported that enrollment was 178 students. The total was broken down by area accordingly: Frenchman's Road – 20; Oakfield – 44; Enfield – 62; Oldham - 28; Grand Lake – 1; Devon – 3; and, Goffs – 14. School population numbers are rarely static and change with the area the school serves. An influx of young families increases the potential number of pupils, so school administrators are ever watchful for opening sub-divisions and economic indicators that might reflect population change. In 1989-1990, Principal Valerie Lawrence reported 145 students, a number that remained relatively consistent as Principal Anne Coffin reported 146 students in 2004-2005. The number of teachers has also changed over the years, but generally they ranged between seven and eleven. Today, however, part of this number reflects the 'circuit' teachers in French, music, speech, physical education and other specialists. In 2016 – 2017, Principal Brendon MacGillivray was responsible for 146 students with 15 teachers and other professionals, eight (7.7 full time equivalent) of whom were full-time at Oldfield. A reduction in school enrollment concerns both school and community as the fear of school closure is often greater than is the hope for either structural improvement or building replacement.

The regular concern of school administrators about staffing, bus schedules, room allocation, financial cutbacks, bus trips, personality conflicts, time tabling, school security, dealing with visitors, and the appropriate use of school time, can be pushed aside by unexpected events. For example, on one occasion a bear decided to make Oldfield Consolidated a stop in its perambulations. During some parts of the school day his (or her) visit might not have drawn undue attention, but when it occurred during school-dismissal and bus-loading, the bear was undoubtedly a disruption to the school day. Principal, teachers, and bus drivers all had to make decisions for the potential protection of their students.[43]

Teachers

Elementary teachers are special. They must juggle the demands of an ever-expanding curriculum and the expectations of home and province to deal with both the collective needs of their class and the individual needs of each student. There are, in turn, new language arts and math programs, skills lists, learning objectives, curriculum outcomes, report cards, and technology to master. There are special school events to organize, meetings to attend and always new teaching guides to explore. Beyond subject material, they reinforce good manners, proper morals, and serve as role models. If they are fortunate, they will someday hear that a former student said about them, "Oh, I remember Mrs. Mackeil, she was my favorite teacher."

Students

Students carry memories, both good and bad, from their school days. Beyond the classroom and their individual relationships with principals and teachers, Oldfield students have special recollections. Among them are included winter carnivals, Saturday sports days, school trips to Louisburg, Camp Kidston, and skiing at Mount Martock. Some recall the arrival and departure of student teachers, others the Terry Fox Run, read-a-thons, chocolate bar and wrapping paper sales, penny parades, and other fund-raisers, and the ever-popular hot dog/pizza Fridays. In the 1980s, students in grades 5/6 had their first opportunity to have band lessons and French was introduced to the grade 3 class. In 1982 there were monthly dances for grades 5/6 and the student newspaper, *The Oldfield Star,* made its first appearance. That same year teachers and parents organized the first Grade 6 graduation dinner/dance with grade 5 students invited to the dance. Swim classes, the spring fling, playground monitors, bus drivers, poster contests, book fairs, maintenance personnel, talent shows, dance troupes, the school garden, writing contests, the fire prevention program, participation in Education Week events, and involvement in school based after-school activities, like the skipping club are all part of their memories. In addition, they recall the guests, including Mermaid Theatre, Lands and Forrest personnel, the local fire department with its big red fire truck, the RCMP, the public health nurse and dental health professionals, the occasional movie, and school parties to break up the school week. Some also remember the twining of Oldfield Consolidated with a school in Fort McMurray, Alberta, and there are those still proud that their school was nationally recognized as a Green School in 1995 because of the activities carried out by students, staff, and administration. For many, more significant than anything else, are the personal friendships that were forged in elementary school that have been part of their lives ever since.[44]

Fire Truck at OCS

Oldfield Consolidated School is one of only two schools in the province that has a fire prevention program. Both are provided by the Enfield Volunteer Fire Department.

Conclusion

There is a rhythm to the school year that beats in time to the passing seasons.

The pulse begins in September when opening day brings both the new primary class, both fearful and eager, and the veterans, especially the grade six class who know that this will be their last year in well-known classrooms and hallways before the darkness of junior high school.

By mid-October the mood of the year has generally been set and the 'sugar high' of Halloween parties mark the passage of the month.

Shortly after Remembrance Day, thoughts, preparation, and practice for Christmas Concerts (or winter-ludes) dominate the minds of teachers and students alike.

The pulse picks up again in January with spikes for Valentine's Day and Winter Carnivals. After March Break and

Easter vacations (and another 'sugar high'), the pulse vibrates with hopes of Spring and Fun Fairs and outdoor recesses.

The eagerness of June marks another change of season and the pulse of the school quickens. The grade six class is honoured for its accomplishments and preparations begin for the new primary class.

Each school-year is a mini-life with its arrivals and departures. Each one is alike and each one is completely different and, at Oldfield Consolidated School, the rhythm continues.

Notes

1. Halifax, *Mail-Star*, Friday, 3 May 1963, p. 2. This was, of course, before the current Maple Leaf flag was adopted as the national flag of Canada.
2. M. Noreen Gray, "Mary T. King: First woman counsellor in Canada," *Halifax Chronicle Herald/ Mail Star*, Friday, 23 November 1990. Halifax *Mail-Star*, "Col. K. C. Laurie, Soldier, University Governor, Dies", Monday, 9 January 1967, p. 3.
3. Diane M. Barker and D. A. Sutherland, "Enos Collins", *Dictionary of Canadian Biography*, v. X, (1871-1880), On line.
4. Margaret Laurie, "Oakfield and its Founder," *Collections of the Nova Scotia Historical Society*, v. 24, (1938), p. 179.
5. Clara Dennis, More About Nova Scotia, (Toronto: Ryerson Press, 1937), p. 9.
6. Laurie, "Oakfield", p. 179.
7. Province of Nova Scotia, Department of Education, *Annual Report of the Superintendent of Education*, [hereinafter *Report*], 1875, p. 35.
8. *Report*, 1945-46, p. 55.
9. Province of Nova Scotia, *Directory of School Sections and Schools in Operation*, Halifax, NS: Department of Education, [hereinafter Directory] 1959, p. 20.
10. *Report*, 1924-25, p. 55.
11. *Report*, 1879, and 1891, p. 52; M. Noreen Gray and Annie A. Blois Smith, *Along the Old Guysborough Road*, (For the Authors, 1987), p. 9; http://www.gofffamilyhistory.ca/GoffFamilyHalifaxCountyNovaScotia.pdf; accessed 4 March 2017.
12. Directory, 1959, p. 19; Halifax Municipal Archives, Municipal School Board Minutes, [hereinafter Board Minutes], 27 September 1961, #906; Board Minutes, 18 October 1961, #921.
13. Gray and Smith *Along*, pp. 78-79.
14. Gray and Smith, *Along*, p. 9.
15. *Industrial Advocate*, "The Gold of Oldham," v. II, n. 1 and 2, (May and June 1897), p. 6.

16. Lovell's Gazetteer of the Dominion of Canada, (1908).
17. *Report*, 1886, p. 12.
18. George S. Tomkins, *A Common Countenance: Stability and Change in the Canadian Curriculum*, (Scarborough, Ontario: Prentice-Hall, 1986), p. 21.
19. H. P. Moffatt, "One Hundred Years of Free Schools," *Journal of Education*, (October 1964), p. 35.
20. C. P. J. Briggs, *Halifax County School Board*, 1932 – 1982: *A Review of our Past*, (Halifax County School Board, [c.1982]), p. 19.
21. Province of Nova Scotia, *Report of the Royal Commission on Education, Public Services and Provincial-Municipal Relations, v. III: Education, Chapters Thirty-Six to Forty-Six*, [the Graham Commission], (Halifax, NS: Queen's Printer, 1982), p. 21.
22. Province of Nova Scotia, *Report of the Royal Commission on Education, Public Services and Provincial-Municipal Relations, v. III: Education, Chapters Thirty-Six to Forty-Six*, [the Graham Commission], (Halifax, NS: Queen's Printer, 1982), pp. 31-32.
23. Halifax Regional Municipality Archives, Oldfield Consolidated School Board of Trustees Minute Book [hereinafter Trustees Minutes], 312-76, Letter, Margaret Garrison to *Bedford-Sackville News*, Typescript, 5 November 1977.
24. Board Minutes, 1 March 1961, #759; Board Minutes, 28 March 1961, #780.
25. Board Minutes, 19 April 1961, #790; Board Minutes, 3 May 1961, #809; Board Minutes, 7 June 1961, #829; Board Minutes, 21 June 1961, #843.
26. Board Minutes, 28 July 1961, #865.
27. Board Minutes, 18 October 1961, #921 and #922; Board Minutes, 18 October 1961, #922; Briggs, *Halifax County*, p. 32, and p. 38.
28. Briggs, *Halifax County*, p. 20.
29. Halifax Regional Municipality Archives, Trustees Minutes, 312-76, Letter, Margaret Garrison to *Bedford-Sackville News*, Typescript, 5 November 1977.
30. Briggs, *Halifax County*, p.32; Ratepayers Minutes in Trustees Minutes, 8 February 1962. The story of the naming

is well known to the 'old families' of the area and was told to me by a number of people including in personal interviews with Peter Thompson, 6 March 2017, who was a student at Oldfield Consolidated School and with Heather (Thompson) Ballah, the daughter of Phyllis Thompson who was a part-time teacher at Oldfield. Ratepayers Minutes in Trustees Minutes, 8 February 1962. Also see: Halifax Regional Municipality Archives, 312-76, Letter, Margaret Garrison to Bedford-Sackville News, Typescript, 5 November 1977; Halifax, Mail-Star, 26 March 1962, p. 17; The early Oldfield Consolidated School Board of Trustee Minutes are apparently not extant but this was reported in the Minutes of the Annual Ratepayers Meeting, 18 September 1978, p. 2.

31. Board Minutes, 3 July 1962, #1174. This was a meeting of the School Board with the Capital Building Committee; Briggs, *Halifax County*, p. 51. Former students remember being housed in various locations until the school was ready.

32. Board Minutes, 27 November 1962, #1278; Board Minutes, 5 December 1962, #1300; 30 January 1963, #1335; Municipal School Board Reports to Halifax County Municipal Council, Tuesday, 15 February 1963, p. 2.

33. Board Minutes, 5 June 1963, p. 3; *Directory*, 1965-1966; 1967-1968.

34. Personal Interview, 16 December 2017, with David MacDonald.

35. Personal Interview, 16 June 2017, with Lois Mackeil.

36. Personal Interview, 27 June 2017, with Martha Mills.

37. Trustees Minutes, 1977-1996, here and there.

38. Enfield *Weekly Press*, March 1988.

39. Ratepayers Annual Meeting Minutes, in Trustees Minutes, 15 September 1995.

40. Trustees Minutes, 1 May 1996.

41. Enfield *Weekly Press*, 11 February 1998, p. 9.

42. Enfield *Weekly Press*, 21 October 1998, p. 8; 31 May 2000, p. 5.

43. The information above, unless otherwise indicated, was drawn from various Minutes of the Meetings of the Board of Trustees of Oldfield Consolidated School, 1977-1996, and the Directories referred to earlier, as well as from

conversations with community members and discussions with Oldfield Consolidated School administration.

44. The information above, unless otherwise indicated, was drawn from various Minutes of the meetings of the Board of Trustees of Oldfield Consolidated School and in discussion with former teachers and students. My thanks to Wayne Barchard who reminded me that Oldfield Consolidated School is one of only two schools in the province that has a fire prevention program. Both are provided by the Enfield Volunteer Fire Department.

Appendix I

Oldfield Consolidated School Principals and Vice Principals: 1962-2017

Jean McManaman 1962-1970
Donald Leslie 1970-1984
Judy Snow 1984-1986
Valerie Lawrence 1986-1990
William Hatcher 1990-1995
Thomas Robson 1995-1997
Ronald Muir 1997-2000
Sarah Archibald 2000-2004
Anne M. Coffin 2004-2010
Kim LeBlanc 2010-2014
Brendon MacGillivray 2014-2017
Kellie West 2017-

V.P. Janice McKay 2008-2011
V.P. Kellie West 2011-2014
V.P. Rebecca Campbell 2014-

Bibliography

Barker, Diane M. and D. A. Sutherland, "Enos Collins", *Dictionary of Canadian Biography, v. X, 1971-1880,* On Line.

Briggs, C. (Clary) P. J., *Halifax County School Board, 1832 – 1982: A Review of Our Past,* Halifax, NS: Halifax County School Board, c. 1982.

Dennis, Clara, *More About Nova Scotia,* Toronto: Ryerson, 1937.

Gray, M. Noreen and Annie A. Blois, *Along the Old Guysborough Road,* For the Authors, 1987.

Gray, M. Noreen, "Mary T. King: First woman counsellor in Canada," *Halifax Chronicle Herald/ Mail Star,* Friday, 23 November 1990.

Laurie, Margaret, "Oakfield and its Founder", *Collections of the Nova Scotia Historical Society,* v. 24, (1938), pp. 176 - 190.

Moffatt, H. P., "One Hundred Years of Free Schools", *Journal of Education,* October 1964, pp. 29 – 37.

Province of Nova Scotia, Department of Education, *Annual Report of the Superintendent of Education, 1865-1960,* Halifax: Department of Education, 1866-1960.

Province of Nova Scotia, Department of Education, *Directory of School Sections and Schools in Operation,* Halifax: Department of Education, 1959-2014.

Province of Nova Scotia, *Report of the Royal Commission on Education, Public Services and Provincial-Municipal Relations, v. III: Education, Chapters Thirty-Six to Forty-Six,* [the Graham Commission], Halifax, NS,: Queen's Printer, 1982.

Tomkins, George S., *A Common Countenance: Stability and Change in the Canadian Curriculum,* Scarborough, Ontario: Prentice-Hall, 1968.

Halifax Municipal Archives, 312-76, Board of Trustees of Oldfield Consolidated School, Minutes, 1977-1996.

Halifax Municipal Archives, 312-74-1, Halifax Municipal School Board Minutes and Reports, 1960-1970.

Halifax Municipal Archives, 312-74-8, Halifax Municipal School Board Annual Reports to Halifax County Municipal Council, 1962 – 1970.

Enfield NS, *Enfield Weekly News,* 1996 – 2017.

Halifax, NS, *Mail-Star,* 15 November 1952, p. 20; 21 December 1957, p. 5; 3 May 1963, p. 2; 9 January 1967; 25 May 1968, p. 31; 23 November 1990.

Halifax, NS, *Industrial Advocate,* v. II, n. 1 & n. 2, (May and June 1887), p. 6.

On line: http://www.gofffamilyhistory.ca/GoffFamilyHalifaxCountyNovaScotia.pdf

Personal Interviews with:

Ballah, Heather;

Bleakney, Hilda;

Grant, Julia;

Jackson, Peter;

MacDonald, David;

Mackeil, Lois;

Mills, Martha;

Thompson, Peter.

(Courtesy of the OCS website)

The symbol represents the Oldfield Eagles of Oldfield Consolidated School.

About the Author

John N. Grant, Ed. D., taught in the public school system in Halifax County, was a Research Associate at the Atlantic Institute of Education, and a professor at the Nova Scotia Teachers College and at St. Francis Xavier University.

He is a long-term resident of Hall's Road and his three children all attended Oldfield Consolidated School where he served on the School Advisory Council.

Grant is the author of a number of articles and books, including Schooling in Guysborough County 1735 – 2016, Mary Kaulback's Normal School Diary 1892 – 1893 and The Mystery Ships of Nova Scotia in the First World War (Cape Breton Books).

www.ingramcontent.com/pod-product-compliance
Lightning Source LLC
Chambersburg PA
CBHW041821040426
42453CB00005B/129